Such Piercing Joy

Blackberry picking in the autumn sun,
A steady yearly task come round again,
Such harsh and prickly work, and yet, such fun!
Such piercing joy no logic can explain.

Wild Harvest

GW00691960

Such Piercing Joy

Selected poems by Helen Grundy

With illustrations by Jane Alexander,
Caroline Hobbs and Sue Whatley

Edited and introduced
by Peter Jackson

With grateful thanks to all those who have supported the production of this book in memory of Helen and in aid of Age Concern East Sussex.

Published in 2010 by The Friends of Helen Grundy and sold in aid of Age Concern East Sussex

Selected from *Poems* and *More Poems* printed by The Uckfield Press and reproduced by permission of Age Concern East Sussex

Designed and typeset by JAC Design & Print, Clockhouse Court, Beacon Road, Crowborough, East Sussex TN6 1AF www.jacdesign.co.uk

Printed in England by T J International Ltd.

ISBN: 978-0-9567453-0-9

Age Concern East Sussex will be changing its name to Age UK East Sussex from January 2011. It remains as an independent local charity working for older people in East Sussex.

CONTENTS

FOREWORD

Helen Grundy was a remarkable woman. Born in Southport in 1917 she spent her early childhood at Repton School in South Derbyshire where her father was a housemaster. At seven she was sent to boarding school which, according to her friend Hope Hill (to whom I am indebted for the facts of Helen's life), she sometimes found difficult 'because of her independence of mind'! Schooling completed at St Margaret's, Scarborough, she went up to Somerville College, Oxford, where she was awarded an Honours degree in Botany in 1939.

On the outbreak of war, Helen was offered the job of Organizing Secretary of the Girls' Friendly Society in the Carlisle Diocese. From her frugally-furnished office she travelled as far as Scotland, with instructions to ask every incumbent whether they had a GFS branch and, if not, why not?

Buses and trains were sparse or non-existent and Helen covered much of the extensive area on foot, walking through dales and over mountain passes, reinforcing her love of the Lake District born during family holidays.

After the war her parents moved to Crowborough in East Sussex and, finding regular visiting difficult, Helen moved to London to work in the GFS headquarters bookshop. After ten years she gave this up to look after her widowed mother in the bungalow at the top of Crowborough Hill which was to be Helen's home until her death in 2007 at the age of 90.

So began her life of commitment to the local community. She became Secretary of the local branch of Age Concern, walking many miles to visit and deal with the problems of old people.

In 1973 she became a member of Age Concern East Sussex Executive Committee and in 1980 a Vice President. Says Chief Executive Steve Hare: "Helen's enormous contribution to our work and to older people in East Sussex was extraordinary."

Helen also used her skills in needlework and craftwork to support countless other voluntary organisations as well as running a children's country dancing club. And all this time she was revisiting her beloved Lake District with her two best friends and, as a committed Christian with a deep faith, attending the 8.00am Communion Service at All Saints Church for over fifty years.

This strong faith shines through her poems, published privately in two thin paper-covered volumes in the 1960s, as does her love of nature and landscape. Poems written over 40 years ago may not commend themselves to some modern readers but Helen wrote in the great tradition of the English nature and Christian poets and those who love their work are sure to be inspired and uplifted by the poems in this book.

In editing Helen's poems I have tidied them a little, tried to group them according to type (an impossible task!) and added some explanatory footnotes (she was such an erudite lady) which I hope readers will find helpful. Her own inimitable use of capitals has been left intact.

May you find the same 'piercing joy' in reading these poems as I have found in preparing them for publication.

Peter Jackson
Crowborough, 2010

Helen Grundy, Christmas 2007

The Poet's Words

The poet's words are like an optic glass,
Through which experience and fancy pass,
For one can magnify and share with all,
The details of the infinitely small,
Or as a telescope has found and shown
Beyond the earth and stars the worlds unknown,
Another turns the instrument around
To dwindle cities to its narrow bound,
Or holds a mirror to the common-place,
Or demonstrates his own reflected face.

Among the rest, my little art, I hope,
Is like a double-sight, a stereoscope,
That into sharp and common focus brings
The spiritual and the earthly things,
By each, through each, to quicken mutually
The three-dimensional reality.

The Serried Summits

The Lakes and Beyond

Wind over Lattrigg

Just once in a while you can feel the truth of the Wind,
   Alone, or with one close friend on the stormy height,
   Where the serried summits march to the limit of sight,
And all but the sky and the grass is left behind.

We have heard in chimney and tree the bodiless cry,
   In vane or vapour or water have seen him go,
   But this is the Wind himself; this is to know
The naked, cleansing, perilous soul of the sky.

The nearest to pure spirit that flesh can face,
   Titan of laughter and terror, too huge to see;
   And this is a creature too, even as we,
Subject to laws of matter and time and space.

This is our kin, work of the Maker's hand,
   No more than a weathercock-sign, a clue to guess
   The ways of the wild weather of timelessness
That would kill the precarious flesh to understand.

Lattrigg – one of the lowest Lakeland fells, overlooking Keswick

Spring in Kentdale

Now ash-pale April's delicate aquarelles
   Possess all Westmorland; green-washed the high
   And windy pastures, fresh as the lambs' cry
And curlew's whistle where the turfed rock swells.
Dove-breasted shadows touch the far faint fells,
   And rainbow light from the uncertain sky,
   Invests the dale with colour strange and shy
As wood-anemones or sea-born shells.

For Easter's triumph did not only slake
   Gehenna's bale-fires, but destroyed as well
   The stark strength of the icy Northern hell.
    Here is no sudden desert blossoming,
    But earth reviving slowly warms to spring,
From that numb bondage scarcely yet awake.

*Aquarelles – water-colour paintings; Kentdale – origin of the name Kendal
(valley of the river Kent)*

The Hermit's Cave at Cratcliffe

Above are bleak moors where the ancient races
    Made their grave-barrows and their strange stone rings,
Among the piled crags and the dark high places
    Whose rocks are furtive and unfriendly things.

And in this steep and yew-grown cliff dividing
    The last green homely fields from the unknown,
Some nameless hermit-hero had his hiding,
    Hollowed his hard home into hostile stone.

And his forgotten hands worked here to fashion
    Christ of the dales, rough-hewn in the bare cave,
With head bowed in unwearying compassion,
    And reassuring arms wide-spread to save.

Cratcliffe Tor is near Birchover, in the Derbyshire Peak District. It holds a shallow cave where, 600 years ago, a hermit carved a crucifix, a niche for a candle and a seat

Lakeland Village

Like those who live in a tourist place among mountains
We are in two worlds; the mess of commerce and pleasure,
(At best lightsome and harmless, at worst a horror);
And, always there, looming in thought and feeling,
The high fells, remote and serene in the sunlight,
Stark in the storm, strange and grey in the rain-wrack.

We are poised between homely earth and the heights of Heaven,
To reconcile them, as folk in a Lakeland village
Find their living in summer trading and traffic,
Graze their sheep up to the crags and the summits;
We live in the cluttered valley, under the shelter
Of high presence, of close and infinite Glory.

Derwent

Do you remember the willow-wrens by the water,
Plaintive cadences purling like spring-water,
    Clear and clean in the drowsy heat of the valley.

Pattern of pines, mirrored in windless water,
Tranced in quiet, like the city-under-the-water,
    And the high hills above, aloof in the sunlight.

And the leaf-slim singers hidden over the water,
Whose song was the song of the trees and the sun
 and the water,
    And all the lost summers that time has spared us.

*Purling – flowing with a gentle curling or rippling movement and a murmuring
sound; The city-under-the-water – perhaps Lyonesse, the submerged land of
Arthurian legend, or Plato's Atlantis*

Potter Fell, Westmorland

Chalice. And Star. And Spear.
Symbols old as time that thrill the mind
With hints of high mythology.
But never is it given us to find
The meaning of them here.
Only accept, respect the mystery
Of that which surely lies behind
The beauty of this wild and lovely land
If we could only understand.

Above the beck's head, here and here,
Where seeping swathes of green
Patch and pattern all the lion-brown fell,
The rushes, tawny spear beyond spear,
Are drawn up in their serried rows,
Waiting for who can tell
What unimaginable foes.
The gold stars innocent
Of spearwort and of tormentil look up
And here and here the pure and perfect cup
Of white Parnassia, erect, serene,
Prepared for what unearthly sacrament?

Parnassia – a white-flowered plant of the saxifrage family, the bog-star

Littleness

I have no feeling for the higher summits,
  I only know them theoretically,
My mind's too shallow ever to encompass
  That elemental calm intensity
But oh! the little things of the high places,
  The trim and tailored wheatear, and the small
Starry and jewelled flowers of becks and mosses,
  And parsley-fern, vivid in craggy wall.

The vast and timeless power that made the heavens
  And all the worlds, by sheer creative act,
Is seen as truly here, in small perfection,
  Meticulous and tender and exact.
Glory too fierce for human frail endurance,
  Terror of utter Wisdom, utter Good,
Is gentled down to mortal understanding,
  And cut up small for us, like babies' food.

Wheatear on the Wall

The Wall loops over the steep of the crags towards Housesteads,
The last precarious outpost of quiet and wildness,
Wind sweeping the bents, and a scolding wheatear
Anxious about her nest in the Roman stonework.

Perhaps we are not the first to grieve for the wildness,
Perhaps some Pict or Brigantian rancher, watching
Hated the earth-moving legions, their roads and ramparts,
And power swallowing up the familiar landscape.

The Romans have long been gone, their names are forgotten,
Only retrieved by late laborious scholars;
Magna, Cilurnum, Aesica, Camboglanna,
Given to ling and larks and the flitting wheatear.

Nothing on earth is for ever; the wild is going,
Nibbled and whittled away by works and houses,
And the noisy swarming of crowds, the traffic and hustle,
And cities eating away the familiar landscape.

But nothing's for ever; even cities are mortal,
Sacked in the shock and sorrow of nations fallen,
Or dwining away as civilisation crumbles,
And the patient wild is waiting to take possession.

Perhaps, centuries on, some traveller, passing,
Will pause by the hummocks of Leeds, Birmingham, Brighton?
Will hear the wind and the larks and chat of a wheatear
Busy about her life in the rubbled concrete.

*Housesteads – the ruins of the Roman fort of Vercovicium on Hadrian's
Wall; Brigantian – in pre-Roman times the Brigantes controlled the largest
part of what would become Northern England; Magna, Cilurnum, Aesica,
Camboglanna – forts on Hadrian's Wall; dwining – passing away*

Roman Remains

Four hundred years the Romans stayed,
   Yet left so little trace,
Their work so spoiled and overlaid
   By every later race;
For Northern is our lore and song,
   Our speech is not Romance,
The Latin in our cradle-tongue
   Came second-hand from France.

A building or an artifact
   Rewards the knowing spade,
Their bee-line marching-roads are tracked,
   And chesters that they made.
They left the turfy mounds in fields
   Dressed stone in byre or hall,
And, snaking over Sewingshields,
   The strong line of the Wall.

But when the spreading fire of Rome
   Had dwindled to a spark
And all beleaguered Christendom
   Looked outwards to the dark,
In Lyonesse and Arthuret,
   Pendragon, Caerleon,
The dream was born, surviving yet,
   The gift still handed on.

From Gildas to the present time
   Matter of Britain grew,
And centuries, by song and rhyme
   Have added what they knew
And still it lends a wild romance
   To sober Saxonry,
This Celtic strange inheritance,
   Our Roman Legacy.

Chesters – walled towns; Sewingshields – a crag near Simonburn; Lyonesse, Arthuret, Pendragon, Caerleon – names connected with the King Arthur legend; Gildas – 6th century British cleric, author of De Excidio Britanniae *(The Ruin of Britain)*

Oxenholme Station

Beyond the bleary station lights
   That shudder in the wind,
The night that crouches round the train
   Is black and bleak and blind.
The stars are smothered in the sky,
   But Oh, look down, look down,
Where glitter in the crowding dark,
   The lights of Kendal Town.

A galaxy of winter stars
   That spark in frosty air,
A coronal of diamonds,
   Fit for a queen to wear,
A swarm of little silver fish
   That swim in swirling foam,
A thousand shining window lights
   To welcome travellers home.

*Oxenholme Station – just outside Kendal, a junction between the West Coast
Main Line and the Windermere Branch Line; coronal – a circlet for the head*

Rooks in the Dusk

Nature

Birdsong

What can be more nostalgic than birds' song?
　　Forgotten beauty for an instant found,
　　Old scenes lassooed in lilting or harsh sound,
Sharp-drawn as in illumined capitals.

Defiant stormcock; April's dingdong tit,
　　Rooks in the dusk; the robin's frosty note,
　　Memory in ambush in a feathered throat,
And heart and mind are overrun with it.

Fragmentary and scattered by the stress
　　Of years, the scattered tesserae of the past,
　　Vanish and reappear, until at last,
Time shall capitulate to timelessness,

And in that victory, complete and plain,
All the lost loveliness shall live again.

tesserae – small pieces of stone, tile or glass used in mosaics

Rainbow

When, the shower spent, the sun again,
Pierces the aftermath of rain,
Across the wild empyrean,
Arches the rainbow's perfect span.
And set within its triple ring
Is beauty past imagining,
Immortal fields that glow and climb
To hills untouchable by time,
And homesteads beyond pride or price,
Deep in the dales of Paradise.
        Perhaps a brief illusion,
A trick of light and steam and sun,
Or maybe, storm and trouble show
What shining calm can never know,
And break the mists of sight and sense
To reach the true experience.

The Seventh Magpie

Across the tawny bents, the soft pale sky,
  For sorrow or for mirth, by two and one
The magpies, ominous and chequered, fly,
    Sharp in September sun.

Each carrying a promise or a threat,
  A wedding or a birth, silver or gold,
But the last magpie keeps the secret yet
    That never has been told.

So, well we know and love the countryside,
  But our discernment cannot apprehend
Its true and hidden meaning, that must bide
    Untold until the end.

And we who share so much, mind touching mind
  In love and confidence and harmony,
In deepest intimacy always find
    A core of privacy.

The incommunicable place apart,
  The secret only to the Maker known,
Who keeps this corner of the human heart
    Reserved for Him alone.

Wild Harvest

Blackberry picking in the autumn sun,
    A steady yearly task come round again,
Such harsh and prickly work, and yet, such fun!
    Such piercing joy no logic can explain.

Unless it be a racial memory
    Of gatherers of food before the Ice,
Whose warm pre-glacial security
    Comes down to us as tales of Paradise.

Before the self-assertion of the Fall,
    When Paleolithic Adam, innocent,
Walked unafraid with God, his All in All,
    And lived at peace with his environment;

Then came rebellion and overthrow,
    The promise scattered and the young hopes dead,
And Neolithic fieldsmen learnt to know
    Sorrow and hostile earth and chancy bread.

And proud piled cities reared their towering works,
    And Eden dwindled to a legend told,
But still in germ and blood of man there lurks
    The deep nostalgia for an age of gold.

Perhaps it is, perhaps — and who can gauge
    Guesswork and myth and truth; yet dreams like this
Show us Pre-history's well-attested page
    Not incompatible with Genesis.

Local Knowledge

I'd gladly leave the wider world apart
To know a ten-mile radius by heart,
To know it with that close familiarness
That makes a pattern of the patternless,
To look across the landscape and to see
Each street and building, river, field and tree,
Having a place, a meaning and a soul
Part of the integrated living whole,
And nervured with the net of roads that wend
Each to its accurate appointed end.
To guess in part how weather-patterns run,
The counterpoint of wind and rain and sun,
And turning seasons; to remember where
To look for bird or flower another year;
To find the present and familiar things
Rooted in History's deeper patternings;
To know all this, nor ever to forget
One more dimension to be reckoned yet,
And see material form and beauty still
Expressing here the Maker's reasoned will,
Beneath Whose hand, chaos of circumstance
Is ordered from a jumble to a dance.

Nervured – veined like a leaf

Seals

There is something about seals that is not quite canny,
  Something science cannot destroy or explain.
We are told that they are aquatic, carnivorous mammals,
  Their feeding and breeding habits are studied and plain.
(But what of the wife who found where her skin was hidden,
        And took to the sea again).

They are stuffed in museums, pictured in illustrations,
  Ringed and recorded, counted and classified.
Experts have written on movement and distribution,
  Effect upon fishing, value of meat the hide.
(But what of the sea-blue cattle that pasture on tangle
        Under the Orkney tide).

Be thankful for Science, and her strict, meticulous servants,
  In middle-earth, nothing can satisfy
Like knowledge, and how it locks into other knowledge
  To show a path of the pattern of earth and sky.
(But what of the proud gunner on Sule Skerry
        And his wife's own son to die).

It's away in the northern islands of Celt and Viking,
  Where middle-earth marches with the unknown.
There's more among stacks and skerries and secret beaches
  Than is ever guessed or gathered by science alone,
And man and silkie meet in an understanding
        That is felt and seen, not known.

In the Orkneys, Shetlands and the Western Isles, seals were said to come ashore at night in human form to sing and dance. If a man could steal a seal-maiden's discarded skin she would have to stay with him until it was regained. 'the wife...' and 'the proud gunner...' are two folk stories of these 'selkies' or 'silkies'. In Orkney folklore the 'sea-blue cattle' were tended by the Fin Folk on the mysterious Hilda-Land, or hidden land; a beautiful green island.

Ash

Ash the austere,
   The grey pagan,
Vassal of destiny,
   Ygdrassil,
Worker of spells,
   That nine-leaved
White wizard
   Aloof and chill.

The Rune-maker
   Is Rood-maker,
Dark doom-fingers
   Hold Peter's-keys,
But the Old Wisdom,
   Houselled and hallowed,
Still mantles the seer,
   Merlin of trees.

Ygdrassil – in Norse myth the ash tree binding together earth, heaven and hell;
houselled – having taken the eucharist

Pirates

Autumn flowers on the windy heath
   Are rascally buccaneers,
Swaggering hairy ruffians,
   With gold rings in their ears.

And the names they wear are pirates' names,
   Bawled across reeking decks,
Hawksbeard, Hardheads, Tormentil,
   Betony, Catsear, Kex.

Morgan himself would think no shame
   To sail with a crew of these,
From Port of Spain to Van Dieman's Land,
   The scourge of the Seven Seas.

The Stippled Shore

London, Kent and Sussex

Moorfields-on-Sea

Wind blowing over the bomb-sites,
  And their low rough walls,
And there beyond like a sea-mark,
  The high cross of Saint Paul's.

Builders' sand on the pathway,
  And the traffic's wave-roar,
Weedy waste under wide sky,
  Like the fringes of the shore.

Never before nor after,
  Can this illusion be,
Once they've built up London City
  On Moorfields-by-the-Sea.

Pimlico Road

If Time, as mathematic sages hold,
   Is one, and all the good things that have been
   Build up eternity, and years between,
Those cynic years, that killed and spoiled and sold
Are all themselves destroyed. And pit-scarred wold
   And lake-drowned farms, and suburb-smothered green,
   Though dead, yet live, untouchable, serene,
All past existence fixed in changeless mould ....

Then, in that heaven of the philosopher,
   Those dreary dwellings and this squalid street
     Are deep wet meadows; ladysmocks and may
     Flower for ever, king-cups gild the way
   From Chelsea's physic-gardens, green and sweet
Across the spring-time fields to Westminster.

London Blackbird

Blackbird singing
   In scrawny lilac,
Under the swinging
   Pompoms of plane,
Lacing with beauty
   The snarling traffic
And tedious, sooty
   Suburban rain.

Kin to that other
   Westmorland blackbird,
Singing in smother
   Of damson-blow
Like a smooth river,
   Forever changing,
Changeless for ever,
   The same notes flow.

Entwine the thought of
   So many Aprils
To springes wrought of
   Delight and tears,
Snatch and imprison
   The northern exile
In memory risen
   From all those years.

springes – snares for small wild animals or birds

Eastwell Park

It's very quiet here, although the silence
Is shot with sound of wind and trees and water,
And birds, and birds, and birds; and the wild voices
Of waterfowl calling across the silence.

All man's work here is mouldering and passing,
The bombed church, the empty crumbled cottage,
The ancient bridge's mossy balustrading;
A soft and gentle sadness of time passing.

But the wild things of field and wood and water
Flourish and prosper; in the stooping alders,
Among the reedbeds and the lily-acres,
And out beyond them in the open water.

And swinging swallows quarter the spring sunlight
Above the tug-boat coots; dunnock and throstle,
And plaintive willow-wren, whitethroat and chiff-chaff
Fill their green world of leaves and dappled sunlight.

So many little lives, busy and secret;
And we can only know them at a distance,
And we alone are alien, exiled, human,
For ever set apart from nature's secret.

Eastwell Park – a demolished mansion at Ashford, Kent

Glory to God in the High Street

We'd hear if we could only pay attention
   The herald-choir of Heaven singing still
"Glory to God" in the High Street and the Broadway,
   Croft Road and Eridge Road and Crowborough Hill.

It wasn't in some old romantic legend
   The Lord was born for us, and died and rose.
It's true; and really matters now; in Blackness,
   And down the Beeches and in Bracken Close.

He isn't ruled by time and place as we are,
   Nothing in life or death can come between
Or spoil the close and living Love that's with us
   Whether in Heaven or on Chapel Green.

No need for pilgrimages! The Most Holy
   Is in our present life and time and state
Between The Half Moon and The Welcome Stranger,
   Between The Boar's Head and The Crow and Gate.

This poem contains a catalogue of the names of streets and public houses in Crowborough, East Sussex, Helen Grundy's home town

May-Dance

Morris Men are out on the morning of May-day,
    Come to welcome summer home, down the sleeping street,
Dancers follow after them, gay skirts a-flutter,
    Young hair, flower-crowned, tossing to the beat.
Blossom in the gardens and a blackbird singing:
    Winter wanes away like the moon thin-curled,
Lost in the splendour of the slow quiet sunrise
        Rescuing the cold dark world.

Gone are the days when our ritual and magic
    Set the year a-turning, killing winter bane,
Roused the fertility of farmstead and garden,
    Quickened the dead sun to light and life again.
Now we know that mathematic movement of matter
    Regulates the seasons, cold and rain and shine,
Far and untouchable as pale sky arching
        Over the sea's bright line.

Yet we acknowledge by our laughing observance
    Science the all-powerful is only outward sign;
Tune ourselves to death-in-life and life-in-death of nature,
    And that which lies behind it, life and death divine,
Knit into the dance and the pattern of existence,
    Vaster than the nebulae, intimate as sight,
Shifting like the dawn-mist, fleecy on the river,
        Changeless as the Downs' calm height.

Shekinah

Having tea out, in a lane away from the village;
The sun on the grass is bright from the night's rainfall;
A brisk wind stirs the hazels and hedge roses,
And our casual chatter ranges through earth and heaven.

Quiet and lovely: but this time, something has happened,
A wind from beyond the world blows in us and through us
Riving away the dark and the cloud of us, bringing
Light and delight and the wild freshness of Heaven.

And every sense is quickened, this Kentish farmland,
Orchards, the roofs of the village, the downs and distance
Are gardens of Paradise, lost meadows of Eden,
The towers of the Holy City come down from Heaven.

The Sun is alive with the Light of the Glory; our picnic,
The commonplace tea and food, is touched and is hallowed
To a rite of eating and sharing, with men and with Others
From ages to ages, the high feasting of Heaven.

And we are a part of it too, our long friendship,
All that we have and love and know and aspire to
Is caught in the swelling singing tide of the wonder,
The Life and the Light and the Love that is Deep Heaven.

Shekinah – the radiance of the presence of God

Brighton at Night

Asphalt and concrete, marine-parade railings,
Serried hotels and municipal gardens,
Jukebox and microphone, fun-fair amusements,
And snarling and rush of continual traffic.
　　But wait now!
　　Out past the turmoil,
Long-rolling, wave-curling, infinite-reaching,
Swinging-deep, shining-dark, unspoilt, the sea.

Acid-blue lamp-standards, bleak and hygienic,
Jar with the dazzle and flicker of car-lights,
With road-signs and neon-signs, fairy-bulbs, floodlights.
　　But wait now!
　　Out there in the darkness,
Tracing their calm immemorial courses,
Unheeding, remote, the obedient stars.

Folk at their silliest, garish and restless,
Pig-people, wolf-people, monkeys and parrots,
Avarice hunting the pleasure-rapacious.
And always a hint, a whiff and a whisper
Of something more sinister, criminal, vicious.
　　But wait now
　　This is the mirage,
Masking the secret, the true life unchanging,
The lordship of Goodness, the Heaven of God.

Paddling at Greatstone

The tide slips down from the wide and shimmering sand-flats;
Towns and villas, from Dungeness around to Dover
Dance in the heat-haze, mirages far-enchanted.

I wade in the sea-edge, the chord of the bay's circle,
Alone in the misty light and the miles of distance,
And the flat sand, and the water, a nexus of pattern.

The small spread breakers, lazily crawling shorewards
Criss-cross with inch-high ridges the bistre shallows,
And chequers of sun-glint dapple the warm sand under.

And the shore is stippled and striped with the tide's ripples
Up to the latticed wind-marks of thin dune-sand,
And the air around pulses with rhythm of sea-sound.

I wade, suspended in ritual orderly radiance,
With it, aware of essential pattern and rhythm,
And the Mind and the Meaning behind Pattern and Rhythm.

Greatstone – a flat beach over two miles long between Folkestone and Rye in East Kent; bistre – brownish yellow

Uckfield Churchyard

So quiet it is away from the lights and the traffic,
Only the glimmer of stars in the yew's black feathers,
Only the night-wind stirring the arms of the cedar.

Who knows how long the trees have stood in the churchyard,
Rooted in graves, reaching for wind and starlight,
Reaching from dark death to the light and splendour.

Rooted in death, but death is mortal and fleeting;
Corruption eats itself out and moulders to cleanness,
And the wind and the stars are safe from mortality's fingers.

And the timeless stars and the wind, changeable-constant,
Themselves are the darkling roots of a greater glory
Living and splendid beyond knowing or seeing.

*Uckfield – market town on the Sussex Weald, nine miles from Helen Grundy's
home town of Crowborough. The churchyard is presumably that of the parish
church, Holy Cross*

Waves at Seaford

How beautiful this chalk-green rolling sea,
  Each curled wave arching to its sculptured crest,
Poised for one perfect moment, high and free,
  Then sprawling, squandered on the shore's brown breast.

You cannot tame or capture pure delight,
  The sudden swelling wave that sweeps us on
In soaring splendour to the perfect height
  For one brief moment, then for ever gone.

Only accept the gift, remembering
  The wave it is, and not the sea that dies,
The breakers on our homely beaches spring
  From awesome deeps beneath who knows what skies.

The outriders of the unknown; we guess
  They bring into the range of human sight
The unimaginable blessedness,
  The timeless, endless sea of life and light.

September at Eastbourne

The beach is as warm as ever in summer,
    Under the headland's sheltering lee.
Bright gulls whicker and swoop and circle
    On sand of amber and peacock sea.
But the sky is softer, the sun more golden
   Than harsher light of July would be.

And skimming the edge of the green tide ebbing,
    Following south the arc of the bay,
Pass without pause the travelling swallows
    By few and few the whole of the day.
In glitter of water the dark wings flitting;
    Wings that are carrying summer away.

And the splendid sea and the sun and the summer
    Will soon be only rememberings.
By few and few the precarious minutes
    Flicker away on arrowy wings,
And the deepest joy and the keenest beauty
    Live in the edge and the end of things.

And the short day ends and the summer is over.
    The sun is dowsed in a cloudy pall
And dusk blows cold with a hint of winter,
    Flowers that wither and leaves that fall.
And out in the waste of the leaden water,
    Wailing unseen, the sad gulls call.

Glory in the
Night

Advent to Epiphany

Advent Sunday

The comforting darkness thins, and the dawn is in sight.
Now is the time to put on the armour of light,
    With an effort like getting up on a frosty morning,
To leave the cosy familiar works of the night.

So heavy and cumbrous the armour to limbs grown nesh,
So cold and hard and sharp to the shrinking flesh,
    Too brilliant to hide the self that demands to be secret,
Resenting the stern restraint of metal and mesh.

Till habit brings new delight out of old desire,
And the tentative flickering flames climb higher and higher,
    And Love enkindles the dreary embers of duty,
And the armour of light is an aureola of fire.

nesh – sensitive to cold; aureola – a border of light or radiance

Unoriginal

Walking alone in the frost and the hazy sunshine,
  Looking for holly, this luminous winter day,
A sprinkle of snow and the air tingles like silver,
  The wonder of Christmas less than a week away.
The bare hedge rustles with little birds, and a robin
  Prinks and trills in the twigs of the orchard-plat;
A conventional Christmas card in its every detail,
    But is it the worse for that?

With regular ritual, cards and carols and holly,
  With family parties and old traditional food,
We mark the birth of the Child at the winter solstice,
  The world redeemed as the dying sun is renewed,
We honour the same doctrine, the same mercy,
  With feast and worship, the same as we always do,
And as Christian folk have done from the ages of ages,
    Would that make the Truth untrue?

You, who would give your living souls to be different,
  Have you the least idea what you condemn?
This is the place where time is knit to the timeless;
  There is no old or modern in Bethlehem.
With the hosts of Heaven before the worlds were created,
  With the Saints in their day, we join in the Christmas song
That sings for ever and ever the changeless Glory;
    Does that mean to say it's wrong?

orchard-plat – orchard plot

Christmas Green

They are types of the Nativity,
   Juniper and homely Box,
   Coming from the upland flocks
Tell of His humility.

Laurel of nobility,
   Churchyard Yew as harsh as myrrh,
   Pine, the singing thurifer,
Worship His divinity.

Holly's Christmas livery,
   Cheerful berry, bitter thorn,
   Hails the Man of Sorrow, born
To win us to felicity.

thurifer – person who carries the censer at religious ceremonies

Star of Bethlehem

Ranging the winter darkness,
   Fierce-flashing in frost,
He is the stern Orion,
   Hunter of the lost.

He is the sweet Galaxy
   Manna-shower from Heaven,
Freely feeding the faithful
   With His own life given.

He is the sure Polaris,
   Sea-mark of the soul,
In fickle mists shifting,
   The one certain goal.

He is the Orient Star,
   And He Himself the Way,
Himself the journey's end,
   In Bethlehem today.

Christmas Decorations

They dress their shops and windows with cotton-wool snow,
But can they see beyond it, did they ever know?
The opal-blue shadows when the fields are white and bare,
The tracery of trees and the live cold air,
The pale unearthly glimmer when darkness has come,
The tingle of the lamplight and firelight of home?

They have robins by the bushel, and holly by the load,
But do they remember by a quiet country road,
The sweet and plaintive whistle at the ploughfield's edge,
The untrimmed holly upstanding in the hedge,
When the cold sun sinking the soft south-west
Flames on scarlet berries and the small bird's breast?

Light-heartedly they scatter their bells and angels round,
Their candles and their choirboys, but have they ever found
The truth behind the ringing and the music and the light,
The singing stars, the wingéd choirs, the glory in the night,
The meaning of the worship of heaven and of earth,
When God became our kinsman by daring human birth?

Nativity Scene

Popular Christmas art distresses scholars
  By the inaccuracy crowded there;
When shepherds watch in snowy northern pastures,
  When Spanish ox and seaside donkey share
A timbered Alpine stable with the Baby
  Pictured Italian-sweet, or Swedish-fair.

The centuries so mixed, Victorian angels
  In dresses almost classical, look down
On mediaeval Joseph, and the Virgin
  With Saxon wimple and Renaissance gown.
And Saracen or Cinquecento magi
  Offer Benares jars and Gothic crown ...

Maybe, but when community or culture
  Adapt the story to their place and day,
They're caught into that moment in Judea,
  Anachronism works the other way,
And Bethlehem is found in every country,
  And any time is part of Christmas Day.

Cinquecento- the 16th century, especially Italian art and architecture

Emmanuel

To some He is born in the solemn beauty of winter,
   Crystalline cold, quick with unearthly light,
Scintillant stars adance to the spheres' music,
   And angels' songs in the night.

To some He is born in the homeliness of the winter,
   Virtue of bare orchards and ploughlands brown,
Berries bright in the hedge, and the cattle lowing
   As the scarlet sun goes down.

To some He is born in the poverty of the winter,
   Duty and death and denial, year after year,
And they have their Christmas too, and the Lord
  of their longing
   Unfelt and unseen is here.

Ox and Ass

Back to the days when the cave-men painted their images,
  Bulls' virility quickened magic and rite;
Winged aggression in sinister temples of Nineveh;
  Warm blood washing the Mithraic neophyte.

Over the steppes, that sent out the horsemen conquering,
  Weaponed with iron to harry the empires again,
Wind-sired, the fleet wild asses, uncaught and untameable,
  Raced like the shadow of wind on the grassy plain.

Robbed of his passion and pride, indentured to drudgery,
  Yoked to the plough or the cart, patient and slow
Labours the ox; the donkey's strength and tenacity
  Sweats under burden from China to Mexico.

But great was the glory that came to the time of their slavery,
  When the Most Blessed chose His lodging with them,
And they shared the secret house of the Lord's nativity,
  Ox and Ass in the stable at Bethlehem.

*Verse one refers to antique representations of bulls: the Lascaux and Altamira
cave paintings, the winged bulls of Assyria and the blood sacrifice to Mithras
whose most important act was slaying a great bull*

Holly

What part or lot in Christmas has the holly?
The Green Man, the Wild Fool of myth and morris,
Nature, rite-revived at winter-solstice
Before the days of Christendom or history.

What apter sign of Christmas than the holly?
Through the all-hallowing of the Incarnation,
The pagan seer fore-images the Passion
With blood and thorns, and the Cross on every berry.

How richer is our Christmas for the holly,
And such survivals, that with wilder beauty
Flicker and hide among the faith and feasting,
Like startled deer running as the sun rises.

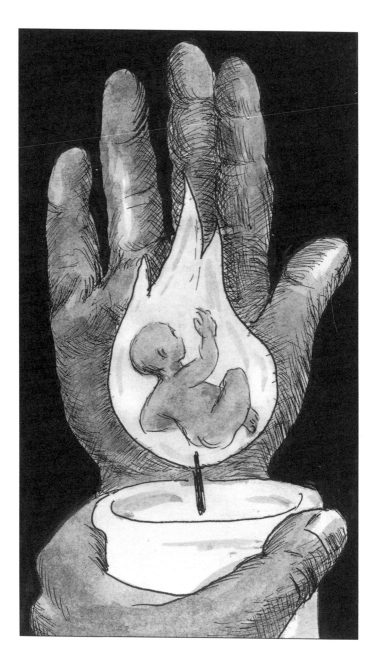

Christmas Candle

Like one who holds in shielding hand
  The frail and precious taper-spark,
The Very Light of Very Light
  Has risked Himself into the dark.

The Love that is the Heaven of Heaven
  Alive and real and fierce as flame,
Made small and close like candle-light,
  To save us from the darkness, came.

And, coming, kindled in the world
  A burning, perilous and bright.
The darkness shrivelled and took fire
  And vanished into living light.

And down the years the burning spread
  To reach the present time and us,
A Light to lighten every man,
  Unconquerable and glorious.

Inside Out

The people inside are settled and warm
   As they look at the cheerless world outside,
And they praise their foresight and money and skill
   That won them a civilised place to bide.

And out in the cold, the lost and the poor,
   Luckless and feckless, scuttle and crawl,
Driven by business or passion or chance,
   And the hand of the government over all.

The man and his wife who were dragged from home
   By the far impersonal hand of the State,
Can find no room in tavern or house,
   No harbour or help for the woman's strait.

Must take and accept what shelter there is
   In the bleak out-buildings of Bethlehem
And only the natives of shippon and yard,
   The ox and the donkey welcome them.

And God in the climax of human birth
   Is born a Man, of our kind and kin,
And in the irruption of Heaven on earth,
   The whole of creation turns outside-in.

The world on its new-found axle turns
   Round the homeless Child at His mother's side,
And the People Inside are blown empty away,
   Lost on the wind with their wealth and pride.

And the Outside People have found a home
   With Him Who is Welcome and Fire and Light,
For humankind is turned inside-out
   By the things that happened on Christmas Night.

shippon – cattle shed

Simeon

I took the baby, just another one
   Whose parents brought him to obey the Law
And pay the ransom for the first-born son

   And then my eyes were opened and I saw:
That this was Israel's long-expected Day.
   Words from beyond me sang my praise and awe.

Quiet in my arms the Lord's Anointed lay,
   And while His mother waited wondering
I saw ahead of her young feet the way

   That she must walk because of this great thing.
Among the servants of the living Lord
   He chooses for Himself an inner ring,

On who most richly is His Glory poured,
   And gives awareness to their heart and brain
As sharp and tempered as a champion's sword,

   A sword that turns and pierces them again,
For who most keenly knows the Holiest
   Most keenly knows all that there is of pain.

The Day is come at last, for me my rest
   For others the beginning of the fight
To win the kingdom of the Ever-Blest

Glory of Israel and the Nations' Light.

The Light Shineth in Darkness

Christmas is a festival of darkness,
   As Easter is a festival of light,
He Who conquered death in the sunrise
   Was born in the hidden night.

Travellers denied the lighted tavern,
   Shepherds watching till the dawn-wind blew,
Sages crossing deserts in the star-light,
   Those were the ones who knew.

And those, for chance or choice withdrawn and severed
   By God's hand from the glitter and the show,
Finding instead the darkness and the Stable,
   They are the ones who know.

The Holly bears the Crown

The holly bore a berry as red as any blood,
And Christ hangs bleeding on the cruel rood,
He whom shepherds honoured, King in Bethlehem,
Is sentenced to a felon's death in proud Jerusalem.

The holly bore a prickle as sharp as any thorn,
When good Joseph guarded the byre where He was born,
And He who slept in swathing bands in a stable-cave
Lies in clean linen in another Joseph's grave.

The holly bore a bark as bitter as any gall,
When kings brought treasures to the cold cattle-stall,
And He who in His baby hands received the myrrh of sorrow,
Awaits in bitter spices the glory of the morrow.

The holly bore a blossom as white as the lily flower,
When He laid aside for us the Kingdom and the Power,
And all the Easter flowers are risen with the spring,
Harbingers and heralds of the glory of the King.

Identification

I was trying to be a part of the Christmas story,
To come with the Magi, bringing gifts of distinction,
And show my treasures, money and time and talents,
But I found the Incarnate Truth, silent and searching,
And I saw me the marrow of Herod, destroying the harmless
For fear they would threaten my hard-won pride and position.

So I settled to join the homely sincere shepherds,
To offer with them the plain man's homage and service,
Seeing myself so charmingly simple and humble.
But in busy bustle I found I was losing the Vision,
Like the busy inn-folk, I tidied away the Holy
Out to forgotten shippons and yards of my being.

Then with Angels and all the bright Companions of Heaven
I wanted to offer pure intellectual worship,
And then I discovered my level; with ox and donkey;
Lumpish, inadequate, dumb, but at last with it,
Content to wait in the Presence, be there with a Wonder
Beyond and beyond the end of my wanting and trying.

shippons – cattle sheds

January Journey

After Christmas the summer begins to quicken,
Deep in the russet fields where life lies latent,
And distant woods have lost the grey of December,
And are warm like living fur in the spare sunlight.

After Christmas the whole world is hallowed,
For the Lord, incarnate in nature, redeems all nature,
Creation is stamped afresh with the mark of the Maker,
And the earthly story has gained a heavenly meaning.

And after Christmas the parable gains momentum,
The Galilaean idyll of spring waking,
Lent's harsh winds, the killing-frost of the Passion,
And the eagre of risen life welling up into Easter.

And power is stirring, even in this still landscape,
For after Christmas, nothing is left unaltered,
The year once turned, there's no return from the turning,
The Saviour born, mankind's saving is certain.

eagre – a tidal wave or bore

The Power of
Christ Risen

Lent to Pentecost

Lent

Renunciation is no grim dark dungeon
    Buried and secreted away,
But a small bright room in the highest turret,
    In the wind and the sunlight of day,
Whose clean bare walls and austerest needments
    Suffice for a temporary stay.

A place for a trysting, withdrawn in quietness,
    Under the scoured spring sky
Dizzily apart from the street and the market,
    The busy world scurrying by,
And out beyond the clear uncluttered window
    The mountains of desiring life.

A place it is for waiting, stripped for a journey,
    Alert in the pure strong air,
Listening for movement, below in the stillness,
    The sound of a foot upon the stair,
The coming of the guide and the marching-orders,
    (How close the mountains seem from there).

Then down again together to the chaffer of the city,
    Duty and sorrow and delight,
And the dull familiarity of daily living
    Shines with the splendour of the height,
And always the memory, the mountains waiting,
    Just beyond the edge of sight.

White Violets

Little forerunners,
  Children of the cold.
White light of spring,
  Before spring's gold.

Redolent of penitence,
  Sorrow and shrift,
Purple shame staining
  Their Lent-white shift.

Bowed as at shrine foot
  In willed humility,
Make of stony roadside
  Travellers' Calvary.

Good Friday Evening

It doesn't matter, weather, crowds or traffic,
It always feels the same, Good Friday evening,
Lucid and pale and calm, as sky-silver
When day-long weeping rain takes up at sunset.

We've watched and shared all day, within the limits
Of petty human will and understanding
And now it's finished, hope and fear exhausted
To passive sorrow beyond sorrow's passion.

And now the world flows in, the household duties,
And people's claims, a hundred things to see to,
But all the press and noise of daily living
Never quite drowns that quiet evening sadness.

Cross

It's a thing continually unseeing one sees
   Not only in ritual object and gesture, but plain
   In nature and artifact, over and over again;
A line and a line at an angle of ninety degrees.

That the Cross was the instrument of the infinite Act
   Surely was never the casual working of chance,
   Straight and uncompromising, seen at a glance,
What sign could better express the adamant fact.

What sign is apter to set for keeps on the brow
   Of baby or convert, a clear-cut division, to mark
   The birth of the living Light and the death of the dark,
The moment when nothing is ever the same from now.

A shorthand symbol of fathomless mysteries
   No tongue can put into words, when our Shepherd chose
   To dare what we never could guess, for the winning of those
Who are marked with His sign, in life and death to be His.

Christ Our Passover

So easy it is to kill a beast or a man,
 To gibbet a prisoner, cut the throat of a sheep,
They have each their ration of life since life began,
 And that once spilt, there's only the carcase to keep.

When the lamb without blemish was killed for
  each family's feast,
 And the Angel of Death passed over the blood of the slain,
The respite was only the little life of a beast,
 And the sacrifice was to do again and again.

The Maker of Life gave every creature its dole,
 Apportioned in frail containers, a span to live,
But the life of Himself is the root and the source and the whole
 That has given and given and still has as much to give.

They can break the cistern and leave it empty for good;
 The prophets they stoned and the cattle they slaughtered, died,
But they tapped all the springs of life and unleashed the flood
 When the Light and Life of Creation was crucified.

And they loosed the flood no power can limit or dam,
 And the Angel of Death passes over the Blood of the Slain,
And Death is drowned and dead in the Life of the Lamb,
 Who was dead and is living, never to die again.

Blackthorn Winter

When the first sunshine of the soul,
   The springtime of renewal,
Is blighted by a killing blast,
   Implacable and cruel.

And gentle blossoms die and fail
   Before the frost-wind's breath,
Leave only stark and sterile spines
   And pallid flowers of death.

Yet arid cold's His servant too
   With all created things;
Who made the winds His messengers,
   And rides upon their wings.

And knows the sorrows we have known,
   And all our griefs has borne,
Who in His highest, kingliest hour,
   Himself was crowned with thorn.

Range Rider

We roamed on the trackless plain of sin,
    Masterless, lost, inane,
But the Lord is riding the range again
    To round the stragglers in.

Alone He travels and unafraid,
    Where the horror of darkness hides,
To the rim of the rational world he rides,
    To trace the track of the strayed.

And the ambush of Hell is beaten and bare,
    And the princes of evil cower,
At the numinous glory, the shock of power,
    That strikes in the startled air.

And the stone is moved and the veil is rent,
    And the cosmos saved and sained,
By the terrible mercy of Love unstained,
    The Lord God Omnipotent.

sained – protected from evil or sin by the sign of the cross

Thinking Him to be the Gardener ...

Mary in the garden,
Wrapped in her misery
Failed to know the Master
  The first Easter day,
Who are we to blame her
Who shy from the miraculous
Deny it or ignore it
  Explain it all away?

Afraid of wishful-thinking,
Of seeming crude and credulous
Afraid of superstition
  And principles betrayed.
And worst — and most alarming,
Afraid we may experience
Height and depth of knowledge
  We rather would evade.

So, when earth is shaken
With the shock of Easter victory,
We daren't believe He's risen
  Though we meet Him face to face.
We hurry to explain Him
As everyday and natural
And say He's just a workman
  Employed about the place.

Gospel Truth

Osiris, Balder, Thammuz, Kings of Corn,
    There have been swarms of gods who died and rose,
But all in myth and tale; where they were born,
    Whether they lived, and when, nobody knows.

When God Himself came here on earth, His stay
    In space and time is known and verified;
Born in Judea in Augustus' day,
    In Pilate's procuratorship He died.

How fortunate we are, that this great Act
    Is set in history's well-attested span,
Not myth or symbol, but a sober fact
    That death was overcome by God-made-Man.

Dear Lord, at Easter we give thanks to You
Because this really happened, and is true.

Osiris ...etc – Egyptian, Norse and Syrian gods linked to rebirth; Kings of Corn – the pagan ritual of the corn king, killed at harvest and reborn in spring

All of Green Willow

O weave us a wreath of the sorrowful willow,
    Though springtime is flowering in meadow and lea,
My True-love is murdered on Calvary's hill O
    And willow, green willow, my garland shall be.

They welcomed His coming with gold palm and willow;
    He rode to the gates, a King to His own.
The trees and the city are standing there still O
    But dead is the King and folded in stone.

Bowed in despair is the weeping grey willow,
    Twisted of bole and bitter of rind.
The priests and the rulers were set for to kill O,
    No justice nor mercy my True-love might find.

But greatest of good comes of blackest of ill O,
    The deep of the ebb is the turn of the tide,
And He whom the great ones had captured to kill O
    Is King over death by the death that he died.

O weave us a wreath of the bright silver willow;
    The gold and the pearls, the first-born of spring.
For Easter is flowering in meadow and hill O,
    A crown of new life for the new-alive King.

Rain at Easter

The dale is full of the noise of many waters,
From the lowering clouds to the sodden clean-washed pathway,
Counterpoint of beck and river and runnel,
And driven rain and rocks dripping and gleaming.

The earth is full of the power of Christ risen,
Quick with Him as the rainy dale with water,
Streaming and teeming with inescapable mercy
In the very air we breathe and the life we live by.

The earth is instinct with Christ the Living Water,
With Love in spate, torrent of Love overwhelming,
Uprooting, cleansing, sweeping away His beloved
To the timeless stillness of Love which is the Father.

In and In

The sweet untameable call of the curlew
Is voice and sign of the northern springtime,
(Soft rain sweeping by fell and farmstead,
Lambs, and larks, and the piercing greenness).

And Spring's return and the rout of winter
Is sign of the greater rebirth of Easter,
Which, dimly we see, is itself expression
Of a deeper pattern of death and living.

Itself the symbol of further levels,
Truth within truth, past knowing or seeing,
In and in, stretching unbroken
From the bird's cry to the heart of Meaning.

And every experience, every knowledge,
In this out-circle of daily living
Is the mark where the raying reality touches
That leads us in and in to the Godhead.

As in Adam

Now God has rent the veil between
    Himself and His creation,
And turned the cherub's flaming sword
    To Rood of our salvation,
And Eden runs where Eden ran,
    And floods the wide world over,
And Christ is risen from the dead,
    Our Lord and Life and Lover.

Phoenix

Just once in time, no mere millenary,
Out of the place of all felicity,
The only Phoenix came on earth to die.

No human thought or instinct could aspire
To guess th' eternal meaning of that pyre,
Where Love fought Death in unimagined fire.

Only the shock of goodness done away
We knew, and sorrowed for Death's prize and prey,
Cocooned in spicy grave till the third day.

Then from that shell, urgent as fierce white flame,
Splendid and new-alive, yet still the same,
From conquered death to life the Phoenix came.

Which we from time to time ...

Time and again He comes to us,
　　With palms and shouts and worshipping,
We spread devotion at His feet,
　　And do Him homage as our King.

And every time we fail again,
　　We sell, desert, betray, deny,
And let the self-Barabbas live,
　　And Christ again is driven to die.

But through the blackness of despair,
　　And poisoned guilt far worse than pain,
He comes like sunshine in the dark,
　　And Easter-time is here again.

Oh, patience of eternal Love,
　　Oh, undeserved Clemency,
To make the heart and crown of Heaven
　　From worst and lowest treachery.

Exodus (Low Sunday)

Glory of Easter is dulled, for this is a time of unleavening,
Reft of uplift and zest, and all but the bare obedience;
Faith and worship are stripped to the arid bones of sincerity.

Past are the signs and wonders, the breathless night of the
  Exodus,
Blood of the Slain for token, the Angel of Death passing over us,
Now there is only the desert march and the long monotony.

There's no going back to Egypt, conscience and mind
  forbidding it,
And the life of unleavened bread leads on to the Manna of
  Paradise,
The way to the Promised Land is across the waste and the
  wilderness.

And the Lord tabernacling with us has never left nor forsaken us;
Too close for feeling or knowing or seeing, that intimate union,
And clouds that bedim perception are the wings of His love
  overshadowing.

Low Sunday – the first Sunday after Easter

Revelation

He is the Way; He has blazed the trail with the latten fire of
  His feet,
A knife-edge path to walk with Him, whatever we miss or meet;
  Not as the Christmas Babe alone, nor Teacher, Healer or
    Friend,
  Down to His death and the death of death He takes us
    through to the end,
To the life that is won in the losing of life, the triumph in dark
  defeat.

He is the Truth, and He rives the clouds as the lightning rips
  the night,
Humanity risen and raised and crowned in splendour of gold
  and light;
  Like the searing searching strength of the sun, like a trumpet
    of joy and fear,
  Away from guessing and myth, the Lord of our love is true
    and is here,
And His words are a shearing two-edged sword to separate
  wrong and right.

He is the Life, the despair of those who mocked and murdered
  and pierced,
He is our Life, and we live in Him when the world has done its
  worst,
  As kings in heaven and priests on earth, with a foothold into
    each,
  We share with Him the atoning bridge of Adam's wilful breach,
For He that was dead is alive, Alpha and Omega, Last and First.

*latten fire – latten is an old term for copper alloys including brass so this may well
refer to the picture of Christ in Revelation 1:5 in the King James Bible: 'And his
feet like unto fine brass, as if they burned in a furnace ...'*

Ascension Eve

So, for another year, Easter-time is over,
   Echoes through the day long cuckoo's roving call,
April flowers drown in silver spray of queen's-lace
   Summer tide of greenery flooding over all.

Spring's enchanting childhood is outgrown and finished,
   Beauty of the blossom fades to setting seed,
Shining dawn of Easter matures to sober daylight,
   Wonder of believing to obedience of deed.

Easter time is passing, but Easter is for ever
   Always and everywhere, Love is Lord of death
Slipped away from middle-earth to Heaven that enfolds it
   Nearer us than thinking, more intimate than breath.

Overcast Ascension

The cloud received Him from the sight of us,
   And hangs about us still, a murky pall,
   A dreary drizzle overcasting all.
And hides the splendour and the light from us.

We saw the shining Easter victory,
   The Word of Light has met us face to face.
   We know that life and death and time and space
Can never keep us from that brilliancy.

We saw ahead of us His Way of life,
   To go out teaching, helping, witnessing,
   And then the smother darkened everything,
And circumstance blacked out our day of life.

Fog-bound, bewildered, blinded, numb and dim,
   So difficult to hold to what we've known,
   That He is still our Master and our own
And this delay and darkness come from Him.

To make us wait His time, in spite of us,
   Till His great Wind comes striding through the daze,
   And blows us into Pentecostal blaze,
That lets the dismal world catch light from us.

Whitsun Heatwave

The more there is of light, the less there is of seeing,
 As in the hot high summer of the year,
Earth is all changed by the witchery of sunlight,
 Heat-haze, light-haze, fill the quivering air.

Quicksilver mirages splashing in the roadway,
 Stiltmen stalking through the shimmer of the sand
Landmarks hidden in the amethystine distance
 Glamour and enchantment over sea and land.

We who are dazzled by created sunshine,
 How can our senses reckon or express
The fiery reality of Pentecostal power,
 The light that we live by, the Sun of Righteousness.

How can we see, or tell about the seeing,
 How can we bring into the range of mortal sight,
The least faint image in a glass seen darkly,
 The wraith of a reflection of the Light of Light?

The Tang of Eternity

The Christian Life

Heaven

Is there anyone today
Thinks of heaven up away?
Heaven laps us here all round,
Filling nature like sea-sound,
Or the interpenetration
Of the ether through creation.
Many-choired Trisagion
Of the Shining Ones goes on
Everywhere and measureless
Just past edge of consciousness.
All our waking days are spent
Under matter's government;
Rare the disentanglings
From the close material things;
Only given now and then
To the minds of mortal men
Here to sense enfolding us
The breath-taking, the luminous
Quiet and vitality
The fresh tang of eternity.

Trisagion – a hymn with the triple invocation of God as holy

Facets

Deeper than the reach of senses,
Real and clear beyond sensation,
At the limits of perception
Is a secret not for telling.

Not from reticence or slyness,
For the Seeing is so private,
No-one else can understand it,
Closest kin and friend or dearest.

He Who uses us for Body
Made us facets of His glory,
True and square to Him, but angled
Each askew to all the others.

Never feeling, only knowing
That this adamant disunion
Is the stern love integrating
The reflection of the Godhead.

Saint Mark's Day

Walking in April storm, facing the blast and the turbulence,
Rain like a phalanx of spears in the hands of a squadron of
  cavalry,
Cleaner and keener, more real and piercing than any experience.

Nearest that flesh can know, to being at one with the elements,
Sharing the quicksilver life of the rain and the wind's vitality,
Nearest to finding the secret hidden in nature's betokening.

This is what faith must be; to brave the shock of reality,
Walking head-on to the Truth, trying to win to the source of it,
Never deflected by waft of doctrine or plausible craftiness.

Blown through and through, drenched, and overflown with the
  power of it,
Wholly surrendered without evasion, without opacity,
One with the Water of Life, and the singing wind of the
  Paraclete.

The River of the Water of Life

Ritual and words dissolve into a flood;
Torrent of holiness; purity in spate;
Intolerable gladness of power unleashed.

Clear, clean, cold, and brilliantly alive;
Sunlight respirable; potable frost;
Laughter and terror and infinitely good.

Will all abeyant but the will to let go,
Drunk with it, drenched in it, blown through and through,
Current-caught, strip-scoured, drowned into life.

abeyant – suspended, temporarily inactive

Rainbow over Cornfield

Sun-pierced the sudden storm withdraws again
And trails away across the blue-dark fell,
And in the rain's last silver flickering
Is born the wonder of the rainbow's ring;
And fenced within the wide and arching fold
Is country lovely past imagining,
The beauty clumsy words can never tell,
Remote and long-desired and intimate.
There is the Promised Land, secure and bright,
On which the Living Water, Light of Light,
Prisms Him through Himself, perfection
Beyond all rain that fell or sun that shone
The hills of Paradise, where holy grain
Ripens to luminous and living gold
Forbidden Adam's seed, except where one
Can touch the rainbow's end and find and hold
The mystic key that opens Heaven's gate.

Tig-Touch-Wood

From the pursuer's hand,
   Children in laughing flight
Run, and touch wood, and stand
   Claiming the quarry's right,
The ancient sanctuary
   Older than reason's light;
Pre-human memory
Of tribes arboreal
Knows safety in the Tree,
The heart and centre of it all.

This is no childish chase,
   Satan himself is "He".
Hell's hunters set the pace
   In fierce pursuit of me;
No help, except to find
The safety of the Tree,
And, leaving life behind,
Run and touch death, touch wood,
And hold with heart and mind
The stark obedience of the Rood.

Here and Now

Here where our lodging is, the sliver of middle-earth,
    This is the boundary, the meeting-place
Between the massy weight of Time's antiquity
    And all the overpowering distance of space.

Out beyond the low frail tent of the atmosphere
    Vaster and further than reason apprehends,
Heavens that elude the groping hands of measurement
    Stretch to unthinkable mathematic ends.

Down below the young skin of housing and husbandry,
    Crushed into the layered rock, fossilised and chill,
In pauseless procession the eras and the periods
    Reach to earth's beginning and further back still.

Good it is at times to contemplate immensity,
    Dwarfing to proportion the conceit of humankind,
Transient nonentity in face of the universe,
    And all the expression of the Maker's Mind.

And then to draw the present like a curtain at darkening
    Over stars and strata, (but never to forget)
Turn to the Now of our love and activity,
    The Here, where our duty and necessity are set.

Psalm 84

Blessed are they of the Lord's household.
We are as fleeting as summer swallows
Housed in clay and of short staying.
Let me fly like a bird homing
To rest in the courts of unchanging Presence.

Blessed are they of the Lord's household
Who drink with Him of the springs of sorrow,
Walk with Him through the shadowed valley
From strength to strength of divine compassion,
Till the God of Gods shall meet them in Zion.

Blessed are they of the Lord's household,
The company of all faithful people.
How can I claim to be of that order,
But might I perhaps come to the threshold
Wait, at call, with His door keepers.

Blessed are they of the Lord's household,
For the Lord God is a light and a shelter,
A house of defence and a shining doorway
Calling us in out of the darkness
To dwell in the House of the Lord for ever.

Ordnance Survey, One-Inch

In arid print of maps, wood, road and town,
    This live, bright countryside I know so well,
That means so much to me, is rendered down
    To line and symbol, skeleton and shell,
Yet trusty-truthful; and it so may be
    That all we see and know and apprehend
Is a small diagram, made plain to see
    Of worlds and worlds out to creation's end,
And dull observance and obedience
    Are the projection on to life's flat page
Of Heaven's dance of pure experience,
    Fierce Love untrammelled by the flesh's cage;
Which map, true-made and followed faithfully
Will chart us to and through Eternity.

St Philip and St James

Join into the May-dance,
  Come and take a share,
Twelve apostles lead it,
  Love plays in the air.

Follow on the leaders,
  Up and down the hey,
Stepping out the doctrine,
  Life and Truth and Way.

Cavalcade of ribbons
  Mingle and advance,
Sorting them and plaiting
  And all in the Dance.

Centred in the Lord's Hand
  Fast held by Him
Through the mazy figures
  Of the shifting rim.

Fast in the Lord's Hand
  Bright the ribbons wind,
Away to the world's-end
  To reach all humankind.

May 1st – May Day – is the traditional saints day for Philip and James

Wheelwright

Do not resent
  Or envy those
Whom the Carpenter
  For His purpose chose.

From the self-directed
  Untrammelled, free
Life of the wild-wood
  He wrenched the tree.

To rive it and carve it,
  Hammer and scrape
Till bleak endurance
  Grows into Shape.

Assembles the warring
  Timbers and grains
To the fellowship
  That His plan ordains.

With searing iron
  And with clinching cold
Locks them all
  In a stranglehold.

Integrates felloes
  And hub and rim
To the perfect circle
  For serving Him.

Felloes – the segments of a wooden wheel's rim

Truth and Fact

Of *course* we remember that Fact is only part of the story,
Translated to meet the limits of human brains and emotions,
Of *course* the ultimate Truth has countless modes of expression,
   The Word has inflections no mind of man can encompass.

But, except to the few and the rare, this is Truth's revelation,
Embodied in accurate Fact; as the Timeless and Changeless
Was born in a named village, of age and of race recorded,
   With recognisable looks and figure and bearing.

Except to the few and the rare, strait is the Way and narrow,
A rigid precipitous mountain-ridge of research and learning,
To be climbed step after careful step, between error and error,
   Away and away above the populous valley.

Uncompromising and endless, a life of covenant-service;
But, the hard conditions accepted, the Way trodden straight
  and steady,
Leads in the end to the head of the pass, and the perfect
  freedom,
   Where Earth breaks off into Heaven, Fact into Knowing.

Mary the Mother of Mark

She never could have known as she went about her kitchen,
   Hearing the voices of the men overhead,
That the upstairs room she had lent them for the evening,
   The supper she had left them, the wine and the bread,
Would be remembered to the world's four corners
       Long after she was dead.

Did she wonder perhaps what was going on above her?
   Or did she leave the men to their own affair?
With meal to be ground, and water to be carried,
   A grown son to cook for, the Feast to prepare,
The days are too short for a widow woman
       With little to spend or spare.

How could she have foretold the days that were to follow,
   The depth of the disaster, the high triumph won,
And from her very room, the young Church growing
   Out from the rising to the setting of the sun?
All that she meant was to oblige the Master
       As anybody might have done.

Braced in
Surrender

Helen Herself

Unwilling Convert

I built a little dreary hut
  Between the mountains and the sea,
Where I could shut the world away,
  And nobody would notice me.

The solid and unchanging peaks
  I had for barrier and stay,
I kept a dinghy by the shore
  To make an easy get-away.

Though rumours reached me from outside,
  Of turbulence in shrine and throne,
I did not wish to meddle there,
  But only to be left alone.

Until the day the People came,
  Triumphant flight, with drums and dance,
I did not interfere with them,
  They passed me by without a glance.

But One there was, Who came with them,
  Whose Presence quaked the rocky steep,
The skyline melted and dislimned,
  And mountains leapt like frantic sheep.

I ran in panic for my boat,
  The stagnant waters of the bay
Reared like a frightened stallion
  And screamed and wheeled and roared away.

And terror trembled underfoot
　And drove me from my hidey-hole,
I could not choose but join the Tribes,
　The weary march, unwanted goal.

What is their promised land to me,
　Beyond the waste of sand and stone?
When never for the rest of time
　Can I again be left alone.

Never again to hide from life,
　And be aloof and safe and free
The Incalculable Numinous,
　The God of Truth has captured me.

dislimned – effaced

Weekday Service

Argyroneta, the water-spider,
Spins his tent at the pond's bottom;
Surfaces to the world above him,
To capture air for his daily living.

Two or three of us gathered together,
Up from the separate cells of living,
Time and toil that besiege and drown us,
Reach for the freshness, the clean shining.

Sanctuary of enclosed quietness;
Voice of the priest, clear and unhurried,
Makes no break in essential silence,
Bright love, lapping like air around us.

Then down to the dark beleaguered duties,
But not alone, for the Light goes with us,
The Air of that other world we were made for,
The breath of God for our daily living.

Eli Eli Lama Sabachthani

Supposing I should try from this time on
To use my busy hands only for You,
Giving You everything I make or do,
Not snatching my own satisfaction,
Or my possessions or silly dignity;
And so perhaps I might in some way take
Some small part of the weight and agony
From Your hands strained and nailed for my sake.

Supposing I should try to follow You,
Away from safety, claims of self and sense,
And with unflinching feet to see it through,
Step after step in willed obedience,
To walk so, could relieve and ease maybe
Your feet, torn and mangled alive for me.

Suppose I offer my small suffering,
No more than tiresome, easy to abide,
Might that perhaps, deaden the thorn-ring,
And blunt the steel spear-blade in Your side?

But even if I touch Your anguish thus
In any little way, my Lord, my dear,
How could I ever understand or guess,
How can I help, or any man living,
The ultimate burden I have made You bear
When You experienced human godlessness,
The dead weight of the sin of all of us.
I can do nothing from my nothingness
But see this shattering mercy for my sake,
And throw away the happy pride of giving,
Surrender to Your love and learn to take.

Vacant Possession

Love-in-Trinity, take and possess me,
Yours am I by the right of purchase,
You have the title-deeds of my being.

Nobody else can evict the squatters,
Rabble of sins, swarming and breeding,
In every room that was swept and garnished.

Dead and dirty and full of darkness,
Until the power of the Lord shall fill me
With truth and life and the Light of Heaven...

Love-in-Trinity, take and possess me.

Tone-Deaf

Leave me alone, I have no part in your singing,
No password into the fellowship of your voices,
That feed and enflame each other like brands burning,
Flowering to flame in the lambent heart of the hearthfire.

Leave me alone, I can only guess without knowing
The purging passion of song, the radiant gladness,
The glory and glow transcending thinking and feeling,
For I am cold sad wood that nothing can kindle.

Trinity of Need

Life of plant beast or man
  Alike must feed,
On water, light and air,
  Trinity of need.

Light beyond thought of light,
  Original, ultimate
Foundation of existence,
  Creating and uncreate —

Living water of Love,
  In passion outpoured,
And the outpouring is victory
  Of the Incarnate word.

Indwelling Power, intimate,
  And endless as breath,
The keen wind of the Spirit
  That quickeneth.

On me, starved, etiolate,
  Oh, Love divine,
Life-giving Trinity,
  Breathe, pour and shine.

Reunion

Here we are met again, middle-aged and older,
　　Scanning altered faces for the friends we used to know,
Rummaging in memory, groping for the landmarks,
　　To try and find the fellowship of twenty years ago.
All of us are marked by the years that have happened,
　　Pain and trouble reckoned with, sins met and fought,
Youth's earnest eagerness is ripened into patience,
　　Less and less of feeling, more and more of thought.

How touching and absurd the things that used to matter,
　　The world-embracing causes, right and wrong so plain,
Never to recapture that first spring freshness,
　　Outgrown innocence never comes again.
But all time's changes can never change the timeless,
　　Cannot draw the roots of the old exciting days,
Still we are together in our work and our worship,
　　The Lord of Earth and Heaven still is Master of our ways.

Now we are met again to take stock and reckon
　　Time's thefts restored again a hundredfold and more,
Deeper faith and knowledge, wider love and mercy,
　　Friendship we never could have dreamed about before.
Middle aged and older, but who would regret it,
　　Who would want to live again in the shallow stormy past,
Knowing as we kneel for the bread and the chalice,
　　The Ruler of the Feast has kept the best for the last.

Prayer at Communion

I take the holy bread into my hands …
Accept kinship with Your humanity,
For You have known the feel of human hands,
Opposeable digits, clawless fingers, hands
That mark off men from other beasts; and You
Have fought all evil with Your own bare hands
(Grim nails for You, a morsel of bread for me)
Lord, guard my mischievous hands and what I do,
That I may make and work only for You.

I take the holy bread into my mouth.
Unless, dear Lord, You watch my every word
I speak sin every time I open my mouth.
You who have been from all eternity
The self-expression of God, the eternal Word,
The living Word of truth, keep my words true,
That I may never speak except for You.

I swallow the holy bread into myself
For only You can save me from myself,
And there is nobody who knows but You
The sneaking evil in the heart of me,
The endless hidden beastliness of self;
Lord, guard my heart, my personality
And make them Yours to think only for You.

I drink the wine from the shared cup, and so
Take into me the given life of You,
To live with You, in closer intimacy
Than kin or friends or lovers; trusting You
With all I am, for only You can know
My mind and instincts and psychology
And make me what I could and ought to be.
Send me from here, filled with the life of You
That I may live and live only for You.

Committee Meeting

We are called to order; the Secretary reads the Minutes;
"Is it your wish that I sign?"; then Business Arising;
The room grows stuffy; we work against time to finish
The unavoidable tedious long agenda.

And my thoughts escape and scamper over the uplands,
Sensing the Glory of Heaven in wind and sunlight,
And earth reaching away to the spread horizon;
An outward sign of the sacrament of Creation.

But I call my thoughts sharply to heel and leash them,
For this is where duty lies; the dragging discussions,
Tangled in woolly good-will, and miscomprehensions,
And one-track minds, and schemings, and bees-in-bonnets.

And yet, and yet, this too is an outpost of Heaven.
If I lift my thoughts to the hills I shall surely miss it,
For the Lord is here; it's His affairs we are shaping,
Inasmuch as we try dimly to help His brethren.

In spite of it all, this is part of the pattern,
A minor engagement in Heaven's fight against evil,
A means and a pledge and a vehicle of the Glory,
An outward sign of the sacrament of Redemption.

Window Cleaning

Wouldn't I like to be
   Self-incandescent, bright
For the dark world to see
   Me, by my own strong light,
And be admiring me.

But that's not how it is;
   There is no light but One,
All other radiances
   Are windows to that Sun,
Their lights derive from His.

Lord, keep me clean and bright,
   A window, where You shine
Through me with Your pure light
   (and always Yours, not mine)
So to defeat the night.

Holy Land

A thorn and ash grow on the steep pasture,
And you can see the holy land between them,
The clear green hills, and far, withdrawn mountains,
Enchantment held and framed in the old magic.

It's real; people live there; I have walked there,
Known the bright tingling air, the peace and cleanness,
I've sown my dreams and thoughts there, and the harvest
Has come to me again, a lifelong haunting.

A road runs through the land, perhaps spoils it;
But it's the road leads home to work and duty,
The anchor, lifeline, watchgate, and without it,
The land is only faery, never holy.

This is my holy land, yours will be different,
Until, when earth and time and space are finished,
Beyond each vision there's the Truth that gave it,
The only Holy Land of all desiring.

Purgatory

We were forbidden such a Romish doctrine
    When I was young; the tree lay where it fell.
No room for Purgatory in a cosmos
    Where Earth hung on the brink of Heaven and Hell.

But ought the likes of me to be expecting
    To be at one move raised to Heaven's height,
Where the great Saints are terrible as mountains,
    Remote and sinless in immortal Light?

Surely in mercy He will give us foothills
    Like Westmorland's green farms, serene and spare,
Where silly feckless sheep can rest and linger,
    And grow acclimatised to mountain air.

So far He's brought us, surely He will help us
    Over the last intolerable shock,
And, death surmounted, we shall know our shepherd
    In the high pastures where He feeds His flock.

Windswept

I'm not as young now as I used to be,
   I have to take more care of draughts and chill,
   But I can know the old excitement still
To feel the rough bright wind of hills or sea
Blow through and through body and bones of me,
   My will abandoned to that other will,
   Braced in acceptance of its power until
Almost I lose myself, almost I'm free.

Is this what Heaven will feel like? So to yield
   My will to Another's Will, braced in surrender
   To the fierce loving power of truth and right,
Reft from my silly self, released and healed,
   Blown through and through with pure and piercing splendour,
   The living gale of everlasting Light.

Nunc Dimittis (Three-Hour Service)

He came among us in form of a servant,
The Righteous Servant, as the Prophet saw Him,
Despised and rejected, as a lamb slaughtered,
  And now It is Finished, He departs in peace.

I am His man; I have tried to share it,
(As far as sin will allow) to follow,
Piecing together knowing and hearing
  And all I can guess of the saving Act.

Foreknown and prepared before time's creation,
The Light of the Nations, Israel's Glory
Was prey to evil for evil's breaking
  By men destroyed for redeeming men.

But What and How is beyond explaining,
I only know I have seen salvation
For me and for us and for all people,
  And the veil is gone between God and Man.

Journey's End

They talk of death as the End of the Journey,
  The symbolism perhaps appeals,
But have you thought, do you remember,
How travel and travel's ending, feels?

The harassment of the early starting,
  Grubby discomfort and blank delay,
The stuffy heat and the crowding strangers,
  Hour upon hour of the endless day.

You are deadly tired and stale and dirty
  Before the appointed time is past,
And the engine slows, and the destination
  Is unbelievably here at last.

The train that has been the whole day's living
  Shrugs together and pulls away,
It's cool and quiet and a thrush is singing
  In luminous dusk and a scent of hay.

And the bad time's over, no more to worry,
  Nothing matters with home in sight,
And cleanness again, and peace and laughter,
  Where friends wait in the welcoming light.

INDEX OF TITLES AND FIRST LINES

LIST OF ILLUSTRATIONS